Copyright © 2017 by Derrick Campbell

All Rights Reserved

Front photo and author photo courtesy of Jason Rossi - jasonrossi.com

About the author

Derrick Campbell is a guitarist who started teaching in 1992 and currently teaches private guitar lessons at Music Maker Studios in Brighton, MA, and also at Noble and Greenough School in Dedham, MA. He has also taught group guitar classes at the Boston Center For Adult Education, Newton Elementary School, and at the Boys and Girls Clubs of Allston and Watertown. He performs locally with his band Element 78 at nightclubs, weddings, and private events. For more information and for extra tips on anything related to learning the guitar, check out his website, beginnerguitarlessons.com.

Table of Contents

About This Book	3
Parts Of The Guitar	4
How To Hold The Guitar	5
How To Read Chord Diagrams	6
E minor, Asus2, and Dsus 2	7
How To Read Scale Diagrams	8
E7, A7, and D6	9
E Major, A Major, and D Major	10
The Minor Pentatonic Scale	11
How To Read Guitar Tab	12
Learning How To Strum Up And Down	13
Basic Strumming Patterns	14
G Major Exercises	15
Extra G Chord Exercises	16
G Chord Pracctice Songs	17-19
C Major Exercises	20
Extra C Chord Exercises	21
C Strumming Exercises	22-23
Learning How To Play The F Major Chord	24
F Major Exercises	25
B Minor Exercises	26
Barre Chord Chart	27
Intro to Scales	28
Pentatonic Scales	29
Open Pentatonic Scales	30
Advanced Pentatonic Exercises	31
Diatonic Scales	32
Advanced Diatonic Exercises	33-34
Extended Diatonic Scales	35
Blues Scales	36
Extra Scales for Further Study	37
Intro to Arpeggios	38
Major 7 Arpeggios	39
Dominant 7 Arpeggios	40
Minor 7 Arpeggios	41
Theory Section	42
Notes on the Fretboard Worksheet	43
Keys, Half Steps and Whole Steps	44
Key Worksheet	45
Chromatic and Diatonic Intervals	46
Chord Diagram - Tab Exercise	47
Reference Materials	48-52

About this book

This book is designed to teach beginners how to play simple chords and strumming patterns using those chords. The basic premise behind this method is muscle memory – your fingers have to learn simple patterns, and then more complex patterns to be able to play the guitar. Therefore, the first chords you will learn will use two fingers, playing adjacent strings. Then, you will be asked to learn chords using two fingers, playing strings that are not adjacent. Then, you will learn chords using three fingers playing adjacent strings. You will gradually be confronted with increasingly difficult chords; the difficulty is measured based on the amount of strength in the fingers that is needed to play the chord, how many fingers are involved, and how much they have to stretch.

Because of the book is designed around this kind of method, the chords you will learn are going to have some very strange sounding names. Please do not let this scare you off, as it is often the case that chords that are easy to play have names that are hard to understand.

This book is something I put together to sell to my private students, so there may be some things that are not explained in enough detail for buyers to teach themselves. If you have any questions about the material send me an email and I answer your questions and then post them to my website. If you do decide to teach yourself, it is a good idea to take some private lessons so you can get confirmation from an experienced guitar player that your playing technique is correct. Also, it is a good idea to learn how to read music, and in particular, learn how to read musical notation for rhythm. I cover that to a small degree in this book, but you can get a much more complete education by combining this book with one that teaches you standard notation, such as the ones published by Mel Bay or Hal Leonard.

At the end of the book is a theory section with some worksheets for learning the names of the notes, and the notes in the major keys. Also, there are three pages with more advanced scales for you to work on after you master the first group of scales. After teaching guitar for 24 years, I can make the following statement with a great degree of certainty: in most cases, people that practice scales will eventually become good guitar players. People who choose to ignore the scales are in for a lot of frustration. Trying to be a musician without doing scales on any instrument is kind of like trying to be a good basketball or football player with a slow 40 yard dash time. I've included a few more sets of scales for you to work on because practicing scales is something that you really should not stop doing for at least the first 6 or 7 years.

There are no songs in this book, but I have included some strumming exercises for the first few chord groups that will prepare you for songs that you'll learn using those chords. There is also a list of songs to work on for the different chord groups on my website, beginnerguitarlessons.com. You can get accurate tabs for these songs from sheetmusicdirect.us and from musicnotes.com. Learning songs should be part of your exploration of the guitar, and you should learn five to ten songs for each section to help you fully master each chord.

Good luck, and have fun!

Parts of the Guitar

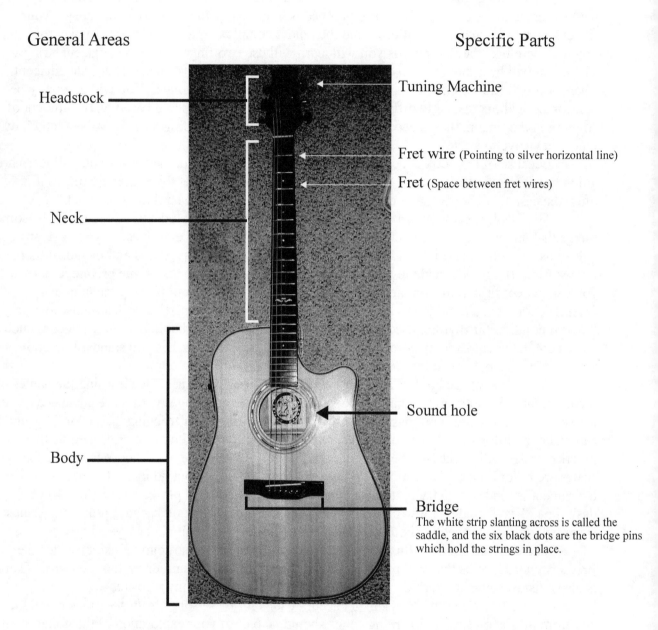

I'm sure you can figure out where the strings are. I will tell you that the one to the far left in the picture is called the sixth string, and the one to the right is the first string. The arrow in the picture pointing to the fret wire is pointing to the first fret wire, and the space <u>above</u> it is the first fret. The white strip above the first fret is called the nut.

How to Hold the Guitar and Pick

There are two ways to properly hold a guitar while sitting down. The first is to place it on the left leg (if you are right-handed, vice versa if left-handed); the second is to place it on your right leg, or the same leg as the hand that is holding the pick. By the way, if you've bought this book, you should use a pick. Once you've gone through all the lessons in this book, you're free to do whatever you want: thumbpicks, no picks, whatever. Until then, use a standard teardrop-shaped pick, preferably medium to heavy gauge.

Lean the guitar against your torso which will make it easier to see the strings. Now, swing the guitar neck out so that it forms a 60 degree angle to your torso. You will probably not be able to see the strings as well, but you will still be able to see the fret wires, and therefore what fret your fingers are on.

Front View

What you should see

When playing open chords, it is acceptable, but not required, to put your thumb over the neck. However, you can't get away with that when playing the F chord or barre chords. When doing those chords and scales, you should put your thumb behind the neck.

Thumb position for open chords

Thumb position for barre chords and scales

Hold the pick between your thumb and the side of your index finger, not the fingerprint part of your index finger. Hold it with LESS force than you would hold a pen or a pencil.

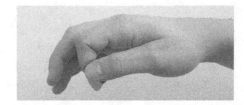

How To Read Chord Diagrams

The chord diagram is a grid representing part of the guitar neck, like a stick figure drawing. The vertical lines represent the strings, and the horizontal lines represent the fret wires.

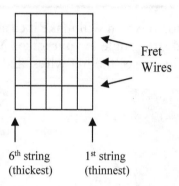

6th string (thickest)   1st string (thinnest)

This diagram only shows 4 frets. There are 20-22 frets on most guitars, so chord diagrams will usually have a number to the right of them indicating the location of the top fret in the diagram. In the example below, the 1st, 2nd, 3rd, and 4th frets are shown.

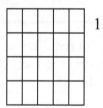

On this diagram there will be some numbers representing fingers, x's representing strings not played, and o's representing strings that are played "open" (meaning you strum them but don't put a finger on them.
The following numbers represent the fingers:
    1 = index finger 2 = middle 3 = ring 4 = pinky

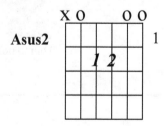

So, this chord diagram is telling you to put your index finger on the 2nd fret of the 4th string, your middle finger on the 2nd fret of the 3rd string, and to strum all of the strings except for the 6th string. "Asus2" is the name of the chord, an abbreviation for "A suspended 2nd." This is one of the first chords you'll learn in lesson one.

Emin, Asus2, and Dsus2

These are the first chords you'll learn, because you can play them with only two fingers. You will encounter these in songs, so you should try to remember them.
For each exercise, follow these steps.
<u>Step One</u>: Strum each chord once, and allow yourself four "beats" to switch from one to the other; do this at least four times.

    Definition: *A beat is a little less than a second, though it can be however long you want it to be. When you tap your foot to a song, each tap of your foot is one beat.*
<u>Step Two</u>: Strum each chord twice, and let each strum ring for two beats, before moving to the next chord. Again, do this four times.
<u>Step Three</u>: Strum each chord four times and let each strum ring for one beat.

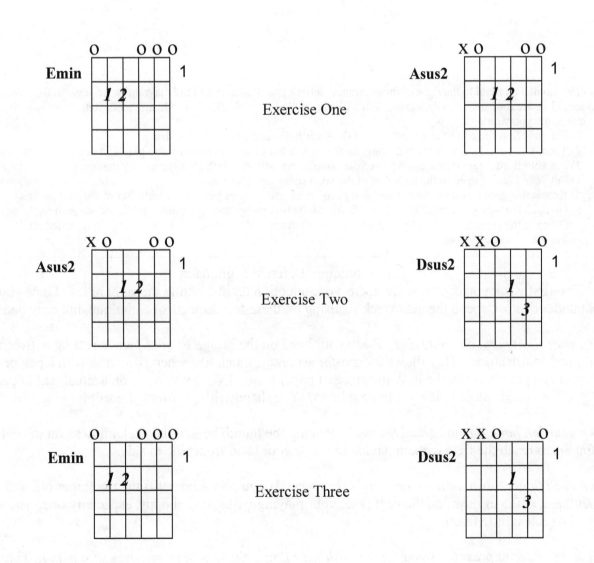

How To Read Scale Diagrams

In many ways, scale diagrams are just like chord diagrams. The horizontal and vertical lines still represent the fret wires and the strings. However, a scale is played differently than a chord; instead of putting two or more fingers down at the same time, you play one note at a time and move your fingers across the fretboard. A scale diagram shows you what notes to play, where to play them, and what fingers to use. Unlike the chord diagram, it is not telling you to put your fingers down at the same time. Below is a scale diagram for the four finger exercise.

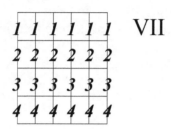

The Roman numeral to the right of the diagram is telling you the top fret of the diagram is the seventh fret. As you can see, there are four frets in the diagram, so it's displaying the seventh, eighth, ninth, and tenth frets.
To play this scale, you would
    1) Put your first finger on the seventh fret of the sixth string and play only that string.
    2) Then, you would put your second finger on the eighth fret of that same string and play that note.
    3) Put your third finger on the ninth fret of the same string (still the sixth string) and play that note.
    4) Put your fourth finger on the tenth fret of the sixth string and play that note.
    5) Repeat this process on the fifth string, and keep going until you've played the tenth fret of the first string.
    6) Go back the way you came. Play the tenth fret of the first string, then the ninth, eighth and seventh frets.
       Go up to the second string and play the tenth fret, then the ninth, and so on. Use the same fingers for each
       fret that you used before.

Proper Technique - Left and Right hand

The first week you do this scale, focus your attention on just hitting the right notes. Once you've got that under control, spend the next week focusing on these four aspects of technique, but only one at a time.

1) *Keep your right hand on the bridge.* Place your hand on the bridge so your pick is resting between the third and fourth string. This allows for greater accuracy, much like when you write with a pen or pencil, you rest your hand on the desk the piece of paper is on. Ever try to write on a small pad of paper, like a 3"x5" notepad, while holding it in your hand? Your handwriting suffers, doesn't it?

2) *Keep your left hand thumb behind the neck.* Placing the thumb behind the neck allows you to stretch your fingers to reach the frets without having to move your hand from side to side.

3) *Keep each finger down until the next one is in place.* If you play a note, lift the the finger off, and then put the next finger down on the next note, your playing will sound choppy, especially once you start playing the scale a little faster.

4) *You do not have to press the strings down with your finger tip, and in some cases should not.* The fifth and sixth strings are hard to reach, and if you press those strings down with the fingerprint part of your fingers, they'll be easier to reach. It's also okay if your fingers touch or mute adjacent strings. You're not playing them, so it doesn't really matter what you do to them while playing other strings, and is in fact desirable that they be muted.

E7, A7, and D6 Exercises

These chords are a little harder, because your fingers are split apart instead of being on adjacent strings. They prepare you for the next set of chords, so please pay attention to what fingers you're supposed to use for each chord, as this will help you when you start working on the Emaj, Amaj, Dmaj chords.

For each exercise, follow these steps.

Step One: Strum each chord once, and allow yourself four beats to switch from one to the other; do this at least 4 times.

Step Two: Strum each chord twice, and let each strum ring for two beats, before moving to the next chord. Again, do this four times.

Step Three: Strum each chord four times and let each strum ring for one beat.

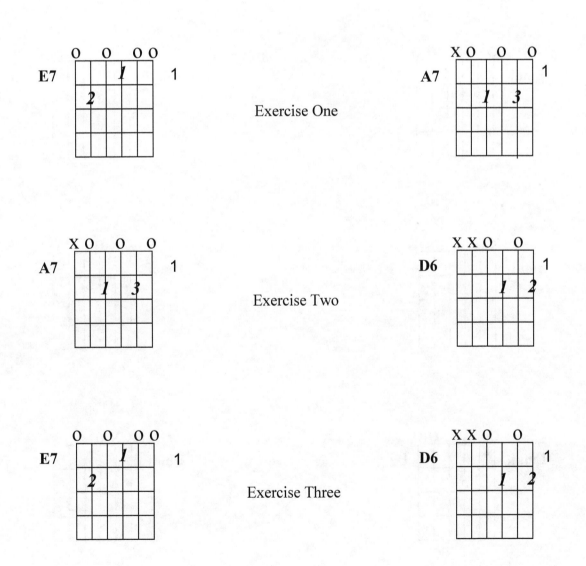

Emaj, Amaj, and Dmaj Exercises

These chords use three fingers, so they're a little more challenging. You may notice that they look a little similar to the chords you learned in the previous lesson. That is why I stressed using the correct fingering for the E7, A7, and D6 chords. For example, when you play Emaj, your 1st and 2nd fingers are in the same place they were in E7.

For each exercise, follow these steps.

    Step One: Strum each chord once, and allow yourself four beats to switch from one to the other; do this at least 4 times.

    Step Two: Strum each chord twice, and let each strum ring for two beats, before moving to the next chord. Again, do this four times.

    Step Three: Strum each chord four times and let each strum ring for one beat.

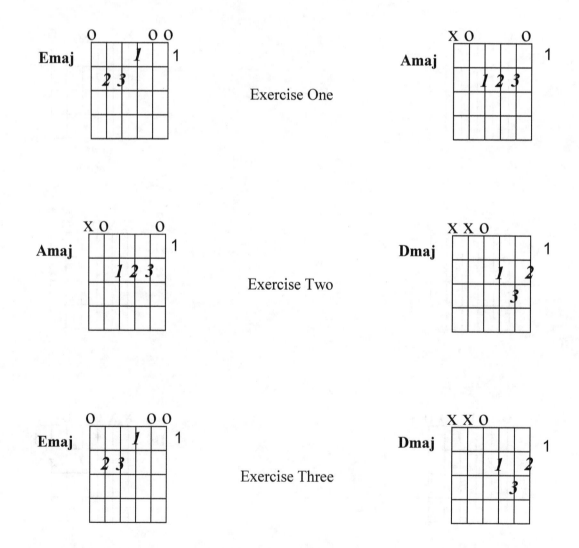

The Minor Pentatonic Scale

The Minor Pentatonic scale is probably the easiest scale to learn, as the pattern is fairly simple. On each string, you'll either use your first and fourth finger, or your first and third finger. Also, as you move from the sixth string to the first string, you start on the same fret each time. The example below starts on the fifth fret.

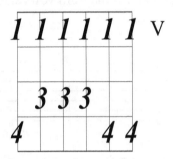

So, when you play this scale, you'll start on the fifth fret of the sixth string, and play that note with your first finger (that is, on your fret hand). Then you'll play the eighth fret of the sixth string with your fourth finger. After that, you'll play the fifth fret of the fifth string with the first finger, and then the seventh fret of the fifth string with your third finger. Proceed likewise with the rest of the strings, and then move back down the scale once you play the eighth fret of the first string.

There are five pentatonic scales to learn, and I present them in order of easiest pattern to learn to hardest. The minor pentatonic scale is also known as Position 5 for reasons that I will not get into at this point, as the explanation would only confuse you if you don't have a rudimentary understanding of music theory. After many years of teaching guitar lessons, I've determined that position 5 is the easiest to learn, followed by position 3, 4, 1, and then 2. At the back of the book there is a page with all five pentatonic scale diagrams for use as a reference.

Once you've learned all five scale positions, you'll be asked to play them in different keys, playing each scale position starting at a specific fret. Practicing the scales this way will challenge your fret hand by changing the order of the scales, and prepare you for using the scales to improvise your own solos once you've become comfortable with them. Having said that, your goal in practicing them for now is primarily to develop dexterity in the left hand, and also to develop the ability to stretch the fingers across the fretboard.

How To Read Guitar Tab

There are six lines, each one representing one of the strings on the guitar.
The bottom line is the top string (the thick one), and the top line is the bottom string (the thin one).

Here's another way of looking at it, using a chord diagram you've already seen:

The numbers on the tablature staff are the frets you're supposed to play on that string; zeros are open strings. The numbers do not represent the fingers you're supposed to use, and tablature doesn't give you that information. In the theory section in the back of the book is an exercise to get you more familiar with reading tab by converting guitar chord diagrams into tablature. Near the end of the book is a page called "Chord Chart" that is essentially the answer key to the exercise, but also doubles as a small chord dictionary.

You will also see standard notation in a lot of books and magazines. The standard notation is there to tell you how long to let each note last. I've listed a few of the common note types you'll see in the first few lessons.

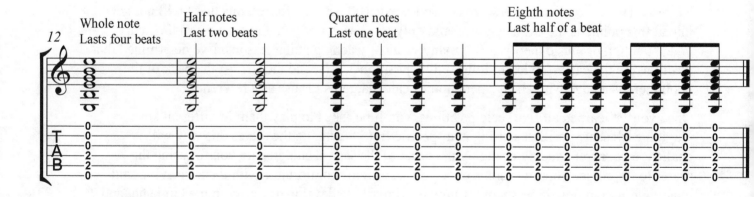

Learning How To Strum Up and Down

Anytime you've watched someone play guitar, they've probably been strumming in both directions - up and down. In all the exercises you've done so far, you've only strummed down. The exercises on the next page, "Basic Strumming Patterns," will acquaint you with up and down strumming, also know as "alternate strumming" because you're alternating between dragging the pick across the strings in a downward motion and dragging it across the strings in an upward motion.

In addition to learning this, you'll also be introduced to the eighth note. Eighth notes are half as long as quarter notes (half of a beat in length) and unlike whole, half, and quarter notes, have two ways of being written.

      Eighth notes as they appear when there is more than one   An eighth note by itself

In addition to seeing eighth notes, you'll also see some symbols that tell you when to strum down and when to strum up.

           ⊓   V

    symbol for downstroke   symbol for upstroke

There is a video for "Basic Strumming Patterns" on my website for you to watch if you are unsure how to play any of the exercises. Keep in mind that eighth notes are supposed to be half as long as quarter notes, so make sure you're letting each quarter note last as long two eighth notes, regardless of how fast you're playing.

Last, and most importantly, I want to draw your attention to the "open strum" trick. This trick is used in exercise one once you start strumming in eighth notes, because there is not enough time to move your fingers from one chord to the other. So, you will take your fingers completely off of the E major chord at the end of the measure in order to get to the A major chord in time, and then do the same thing on the last upstroke of the A major chord so you get back to the E major chord by the 1st beat. This trick is also used in exercises 5, 6, 8, and 9. You don't have to hit the exact open strings specified in the tablature; if you hit the open fourth, third, and second string instead of the third, second and first, that is okay and not a mistake. It's not important what strings you hit as long as you continue strumming.

Basic Strumming Patterns

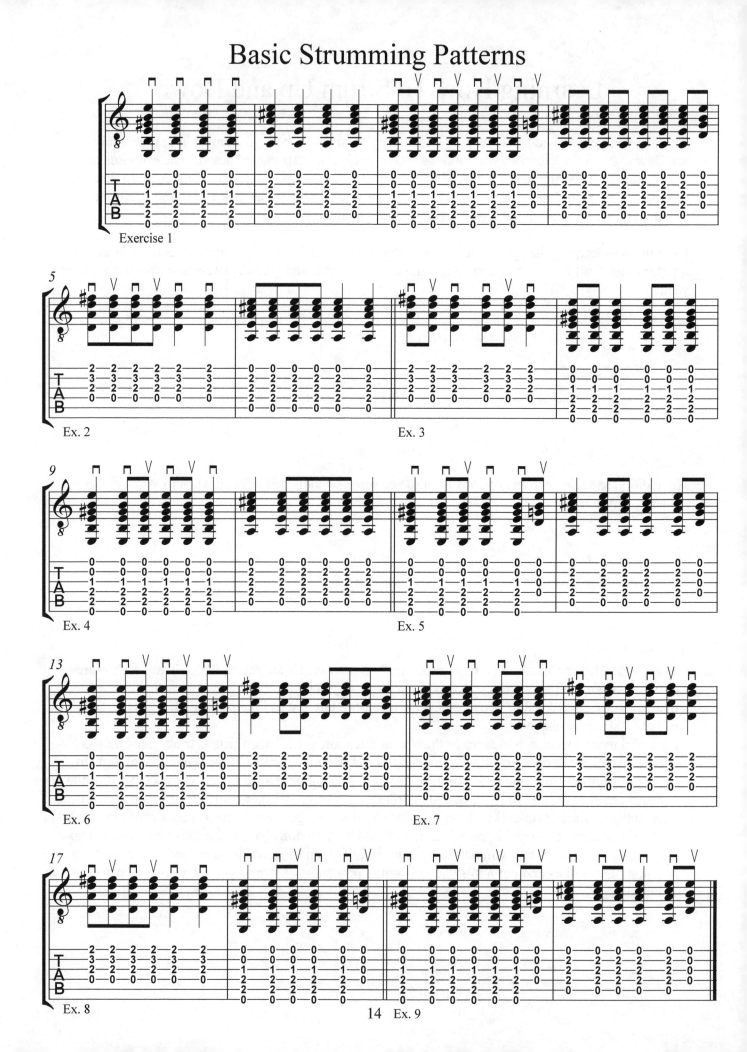

Gmaj Exercises

The layout of this page is a little different from the previous exercises. For each step, you'll practice going from the G chord "fragment" to the Amaj chord in whole, half and quarter notes, and then to the Dmaj chord in whole, half and quarter notes. Step 1 is really Step 1a - going from G6 to Amaj - and Step 1b - going from G6 to Dmaj.

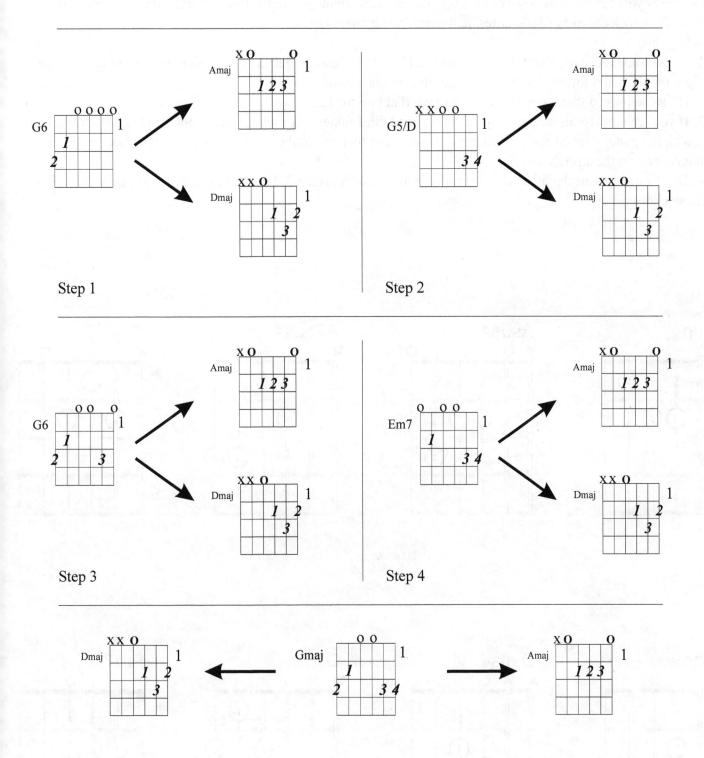

Extra G Chord Exercises

These are chords you should work on learning after mastering the G chord, as you will run into them in some the songs you'll learn in the G chord group. Do the same thing you did with the G exercises and practice switch from G to each chord in whole notes, half notes, and quarter notes.
A few tips:
1. Take note of A7sus4, Cadd 9, Dsus4, and Em7, as those chords get used a lot with the four finger version of (since the third and fourth finger stay on the same notes.
2. B7 is the most difficult one to master so save that one for last.
3. If you have problems stretching your second and third finger apart when you try the Em7 chord, practice doin it with the guitar capoed at the third fret or higher, and then move the capo down a fret each week until your fingers can do the stretch.
4. Don't forget about the other chords you've learned like Asus2, A7, Dsus2, Em, and E7, as you will run into those chords again.

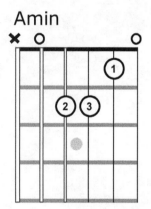
Amin

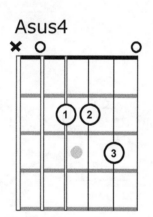
Asus4

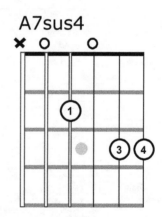
A7sus4

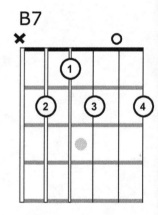
B7

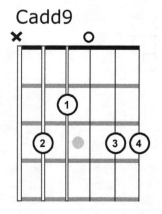
Cadd9

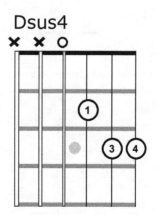
Dsus4

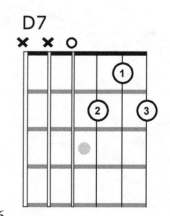
D7

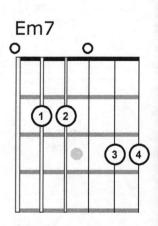
Em7

G Chord Practice Songs

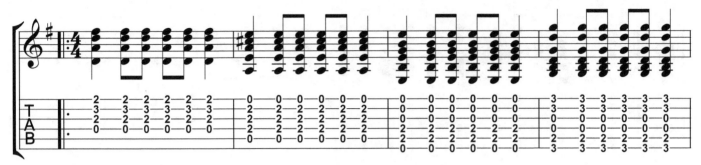

Example Song 1

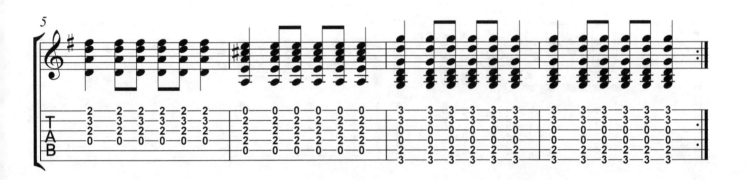

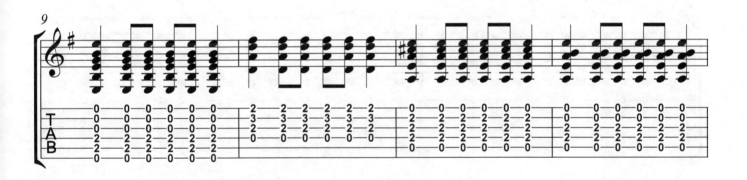

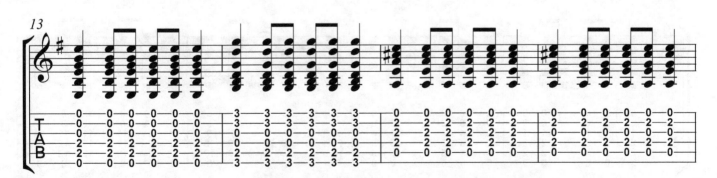

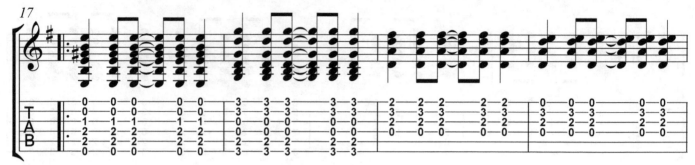

Example Song 2

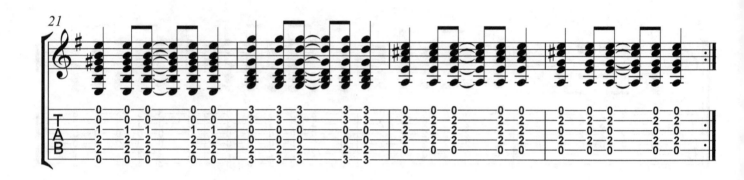

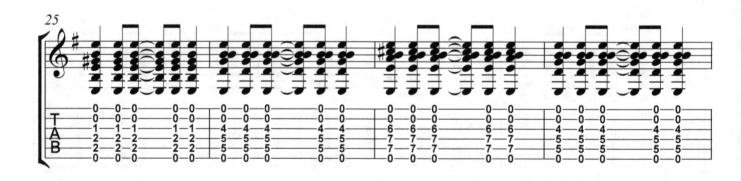

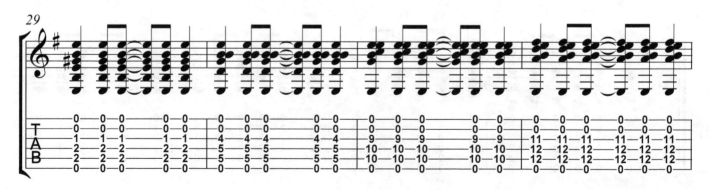

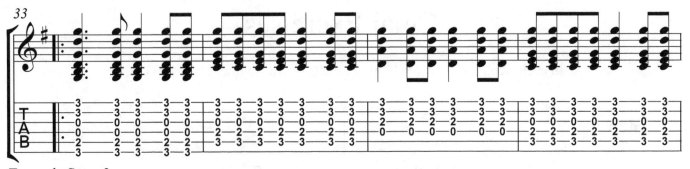

Example Song 3

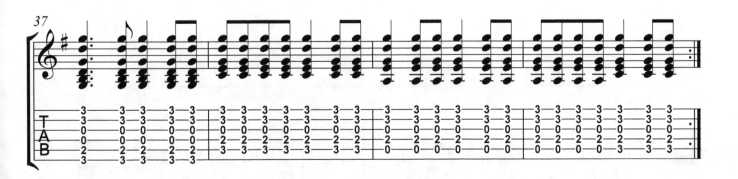

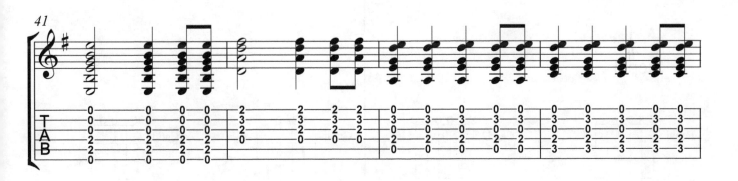

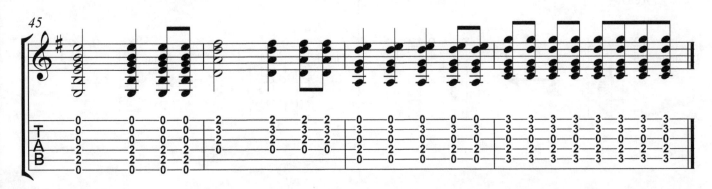

Cmaj Exercises

In each step, you'll switch between the C chord fragment to D or G.

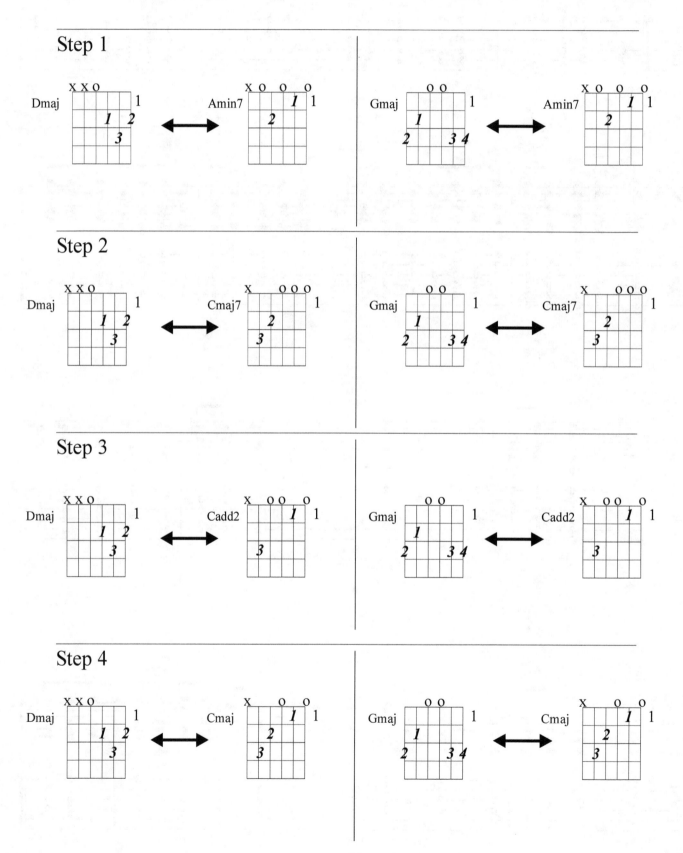

Extra C Chord Exercises

These are chords you should work on learning after mastering the C chord, as you will run into them in some of the songs you'll learn in the C chord group. Do the same thing you did with the C exercises and practice switching from C to each chord in whole notes, half notes, and quarter notes.
A few tips:
1. Practice the two Amin7 chords to G and D rather than C. Going from C to Amin 7 is really easy.
2. Also, do C - C/B - Am as C/B only gets used between C and Am. Work on G - C7, C (extra G) to Fadd9
    as well as there are some songs that I recommend learning that use those chord changes
3. It's a good idea to also work on switching from C to some of the chords from the extra G chord exercises.
    Practice C to Am, B7, D7, Em, and Em7, and Fmaj7.

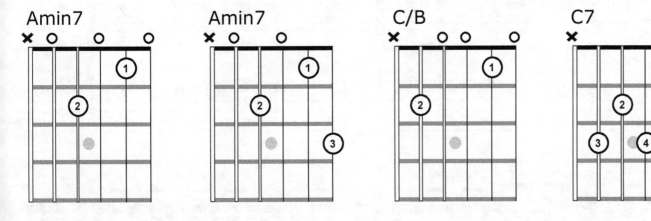

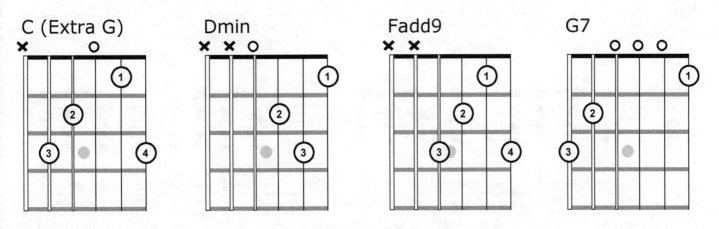

C Chord Strumming Exercises

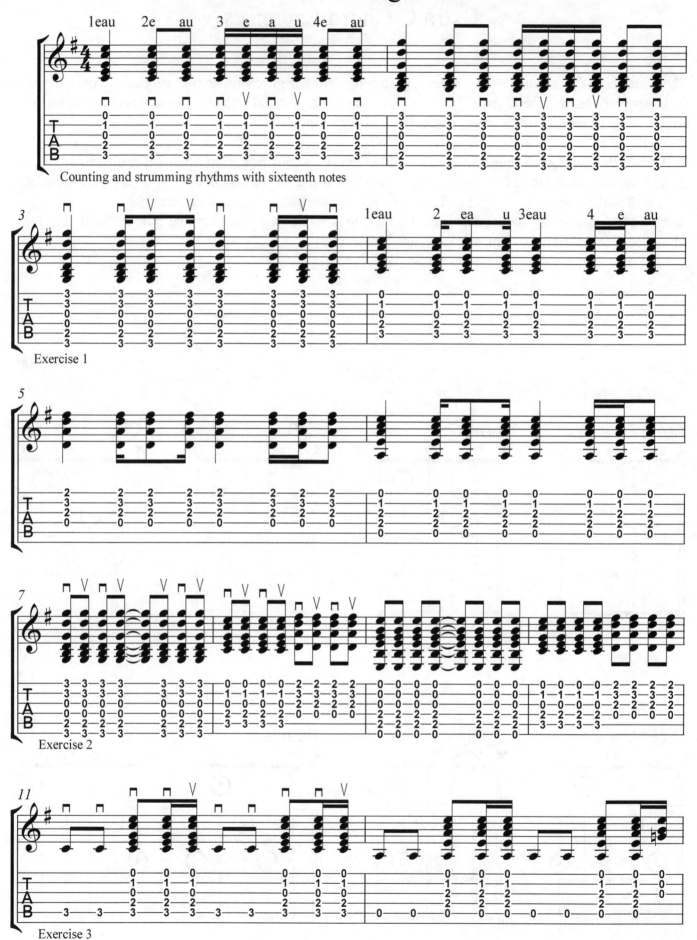

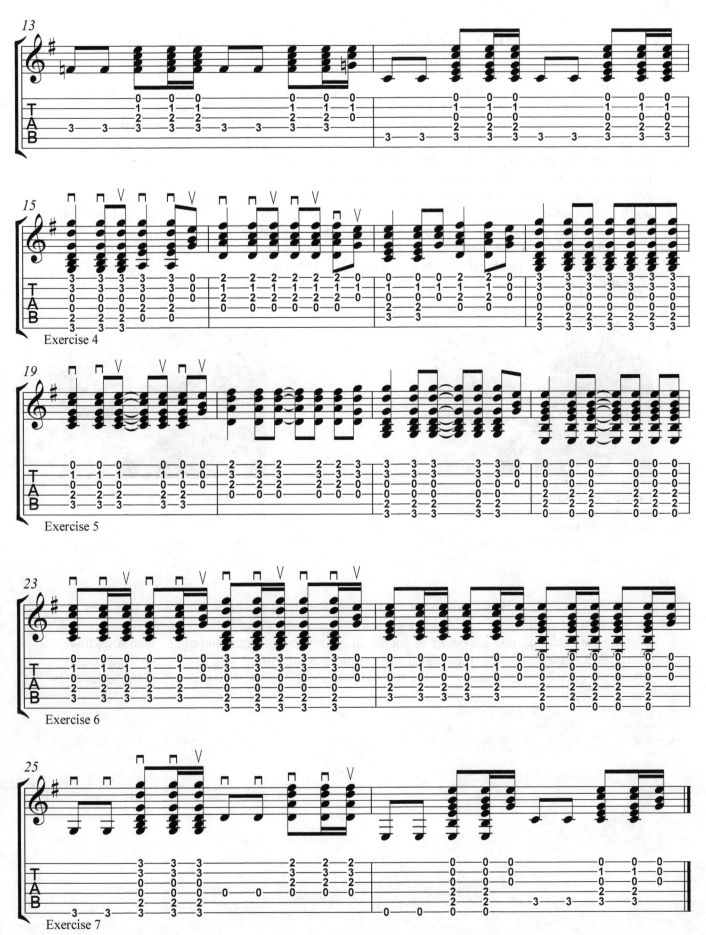

How To Play The F Major Chord

The F Major chord is a little trickier than the other chords you've learned, because you have to lay your index finger across the first and second string. Also, you have to be a little more careful about pressing on the strings with your fingertips, and not letting your fingers touch the adjacent strings, as doing so will result in some muting of the strings. As if that isn't enough to worry about, you also need to put your thumb behind the neck for this chord. Putting your thumb behind the neck will make it easier to exert extra pressure to press the two strings down with your first finger, and will also allow you to get your fingers in a more upright position so they don't mute adjacent strings. It will also prepare you for the next chord, B Minor, which is a full barre chord (i.e. you have to lay your index finger across five strings).

It's important to watch your elbow's position for this chord; keeping your elbow against your torso will force your fret hand fingers into a position where muting is less likely to occur. Take a look at the pictures below.

F chord played correctly. Note elbow position and how the guitar neck is not parallel to the torso.

F chord played incorrectly. The elbow is not held against the torso.

It is possible to play F with your thumb over the top of the neck, but I have all of my students play it with the thumb behind the neck because that prepares them for the next step of learning barre chords, and it's easier to get the finger placement right and get a clean sounding chord. After you've mastered the chord and get more comfortable with it, you may find you're able to play it with your thumb over the top of the neck. For now, though, stick to the techniques I've described.

Fmaj Exercises

There are five steps to learning the F chord, although some people find it easier to skip the Fsus2 exercise and just go straight from the Dm7 step to the Fmaj chord. In each step, switch between the F fragment to Cmaj and Gmaj in whole notes, half notes, and quarter notes. Also, since this chord involves laying your index finger across the first and second strings, you need to put your thumb behind the neck.

Fmaj7

Step One
Keep your elbow against your torso, as this will put your hand and fingers in the correct position so your fingers are "leaning" toward the headstock.

Dmin11

Step Two
Lay your index finger across the first and second strings. Press the strings down with the side of the index finger (the "thumb" side).

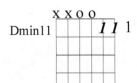
Dmin7

Step Three
Add the second finger, and try to make it lean toward the headstock.

Fsus2

Step Four
Add the third finger. Don't worry if it mutes the third string a little bit

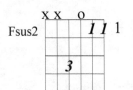
Fmaj

Step Five
You might also try switching to the Dmin chord in addition to Cmaj and Gmaj.

B Minor Exercises

B minor is a "barre" chord, which means you lay your index finger across most of the strings. To do these types of chords you need to develop a lot of strength in your fingers, and also get used to really putting your thumb behind the neck. As you did with the F chord, you need to have your elbow close to your torso to get your fingers to lean the correct way. For each step, practice switching between the Bmin fragment to G, C, A, and D.

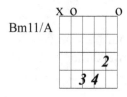

Bm11/A

Step One:
With this exercise, you're practicing switching the thumb placement from the open chord position to the barre chord position.

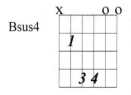

Bsus4

Step Two:
Master the stretch. This stretch between the first and third finger can slow you down, and this exercise isolates that movement.

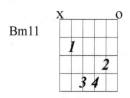

Bm11

Step Three
Now try to get all four fingers down. Stretching the first and second fingers apart can be kind of tricky.

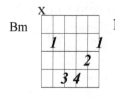

Bm

Step Four
Master the barre, and you've got it. Once you're comfortable with this, you should try to position your first finger so it touches the sixth string and mutes it.

Once you've mastered this chord, you will have developed enough strength in your fingers to learn the other barre chords without too much difficulty, except for "root 5 major chords" such as B Major. To play those chords, you have to lay your third finger across three strings, in addition to laying the first finger across five strings. Give yourself a few months of playing songs with the B Minor chord before attempting the B Major chord.

Barre Chords

These are the other barre chords you'll need to learn once you master the B minor chord. There are two types: chords with a root note (i.e. the lowest note) on the 6th string, and chords with a root on the 5th string. Once you've learned B minor - the root 5 version - you should then try the root 6 major barre chord, as the pattern is very similar, then try learning the root 6 minor chord. The last one to try is the root 5 major chord, and that is the hardest one. You have to be able to bend the last digit on your third finger backwards a little to play that chord.

Root 6 Barre Chords

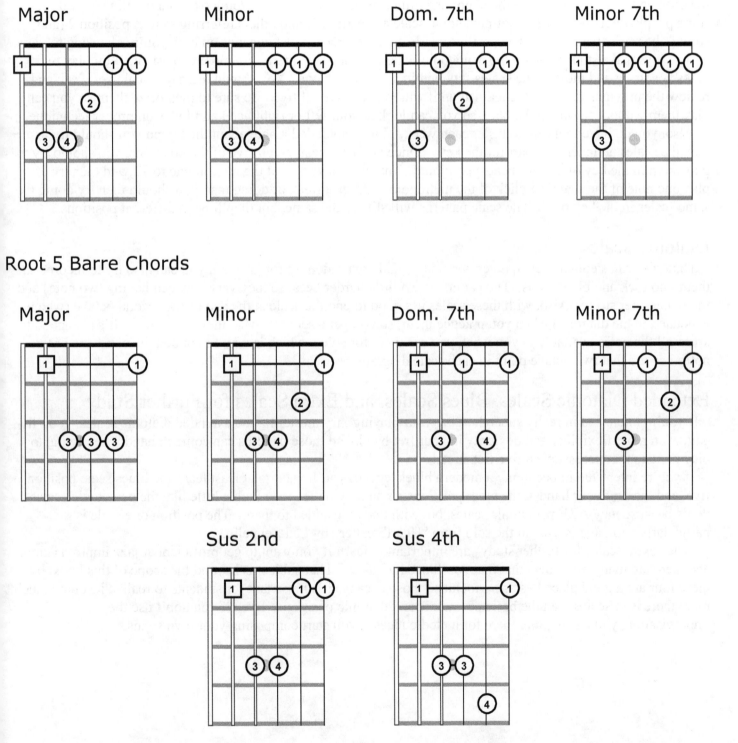

Root 5 Barre Chords

Scales

Practicing scales is a really important part of developing your ability to play the guitar. In addition to preparing you to learn songs with guitar riffs, the muscle memory you develop to master scales will help your ability to switch from one chord to another. Eventually, you can also use these scales to improvise your own guitar solos or write your own songs if you're so inclined.

Pentatonic Scales

Pentatonic scales are used mostly in blues and rock guitar solos and riffs. There are five scales to learn, but the ones you'll use the most are the major and minor pentatonic scales. If you look around online, you'll see some people referring to the major pentatonic scale as position 1, and others referring to it as position 2 (and calling the minor pentatonic scale position 1). Both are correct, it just depends on how you're choosing to view.
I always make students learn the pentatonic scales first as the patterns are more consistent. You play two notes per string and most of the scales stay within a four fret range. You should learn one scale per week and review the previous ones you've learned until you've mastered all five. Be sure to memorize them so you can play them without staring at the book so you can look at your left or right hand and focus on proper technique.
Also, you do have to try to go faster each week. I have included a note about the tempo you should try to play the scales at under the chart for the keys. Once you have learned all five of the positions, you should try to play them in the key of C at 72 beats per minute. That means you'll set the metronome to 72, and then try to play one note of the scale per click of the metronome. After a week of doing that, you should then try doing the same scales in the key of G. The scale patterns will still be the same, but they'll be in different positions.

Diatonic Scales

Diatonic scales contain seven notes per octave, and are used more for jazz, but you can also try to incorporate them into rock and blues solos. The patterns are a little harder because they vary between having two notes and three notes per string. Also, with these scales it's good to end the scale at the end of the second octave (which is notated in the diagram) when you practice them, so you get a sense of what they sound like. It's also good to know all the notes available to you when you use them for solos, which is why I included the extra one or two notes beyond that two octave point in each scale diagram.

Extended Diatonic Scales, Blues Scales, and Extra Scales for Further Study

If you're interested in really supercharging your playing, try mastering the extended diatonic scales. You'll gain even more flexibility and dexterity in your fret hand, and those patterns can come in hand when trying to play phrases that necessitate a five fret stretch.
If you're interested in becoming a modern blues legend, you'll want to at least learn the blues scale position five, and then try your hand at the other positions. You may notice they look a little like the pentatonic scales - that's because they ARE pentatonic scales, but with one note added to them. The position one scale is particularly cool, and is used in the solo from "Heartbreaker" by Led Zeppelin.
The "extra scales for further study" are important to learn if you want to get proficient at jazz improvisation, and there are many more than that that you'll need to know. That subject is beyond the scope of this book, but these four are a good place to start. I included those because it's important for students to realize just how much more there is to scales than the basic pentatonic and diatonic positions. Even if you don't use them for improvisation, you can explore them for melodic ideas if you start composing your own songs.

Pentatonic Scales

Major (Pos. 1)
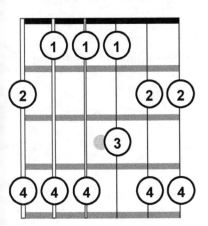

Position 2
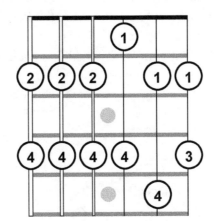

Position 3
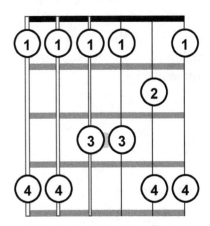

Position 4
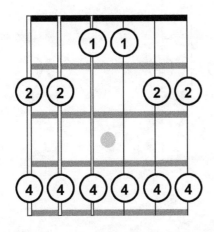

Minor (Pos. 5)
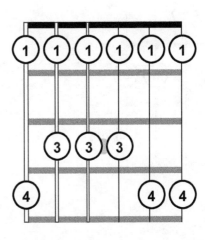

Key of...	C	G	D	A	E	B	F#	C#	Ab	Eb	Bb	F
Position 1	8	3	10	5	12	7	2	9	4	11	6	13
Position 2	10	5	12	7	2	9	4	11	6	13	8	3
Position 3	12	7	2	9	4	11	6	1	8	3	10	5
Position 4	3	10	5	12	7	2	9	4	11	6	13	8
Position 5	5	12	7	2	9	4	11	6	1	8	3	10
Tempo	66	72	80	88	96	104	112	120	126	132	140	148

The numbers in this chart are where the first note of the scale starts. So, for example, in the key of C, you would play the Major scale with your 2nd finger on the 8th fret, and the Position 2 scale with your 2nd finger on the 10th fret. The Minor scale in the key of C would be played with your 1st finger on the 5th fret.

Pentatonic Scales in the Open Position

If you're playing an acoustic guitar without a cutaway, there's often going to be one pentatonic scale you won't be able to do because it's up at the thirteenth fret or higher. If that's the case, you can use one of these scales instead. The position 1 scale is used in the key of F, position 2 in the key of E flat, position 3 in the key of C, position 4 in the key of B flat, and position 5 in the key of G. There are two versions of the position 5 scale, each with different fingerings. Try learning both ways, as you'll find each one is useful depending on what song you're playing.

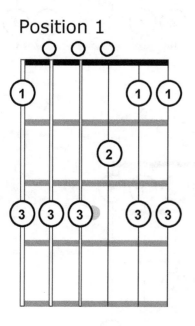
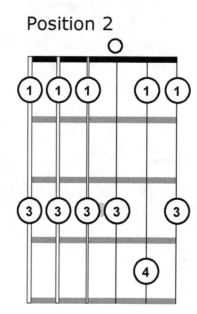
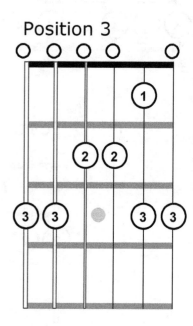
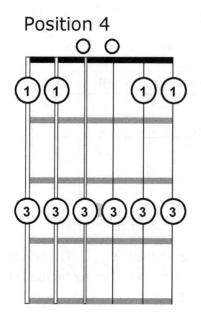
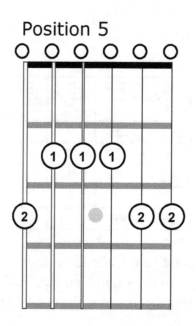
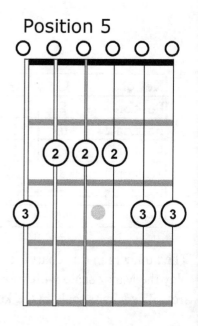

Advanced Pentatonic Exercises

Diatonic Modes

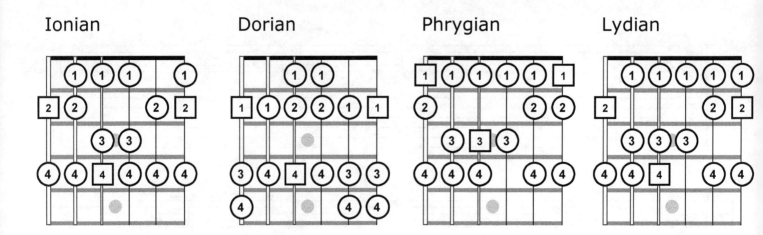

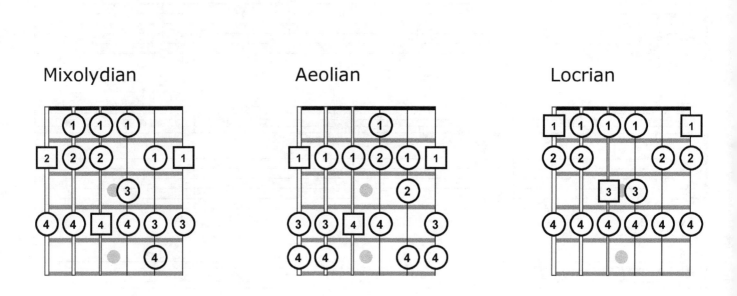

Key of...	C	G	D	A	E	B	F#	C#	Ab	Eb	Bb	F
Ionian	8	3	10	5	12	7	2	9	4	11	6	13/1
Dorian	10	5	12	7	2	9	4	11	6	13/1	8	3
Phrygian	12	7	2	9	4	11	6	13/1	8	3	10	5
Lydian	13/1	8	3	10	5	12	7	2	9	4	11	6
Mixolydian	3	10	5	12	7	2	9	4	11	6	13/1	8
Aeolian	5	12	7	2	9	4	11	6	13/1	8	3	10
Locrian	7	2	9	4	11	6	13/1	8	3	10	5	12
Tempo	66	72	80	88	96	104	112	120	126	132	140	148

Advanced Diatonic Exercises

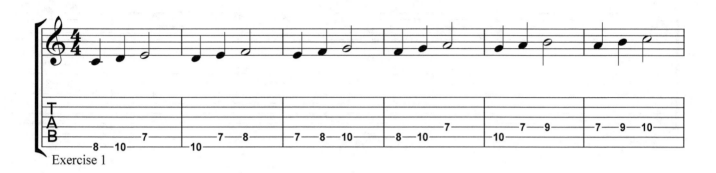
Exercise 1

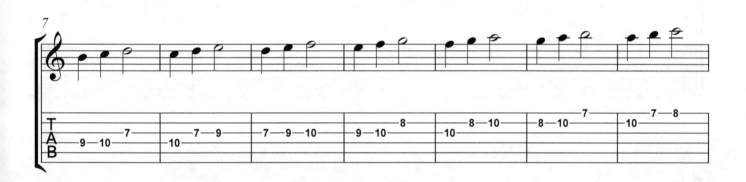

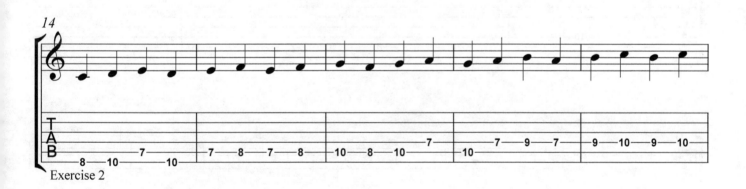
Exercise 2

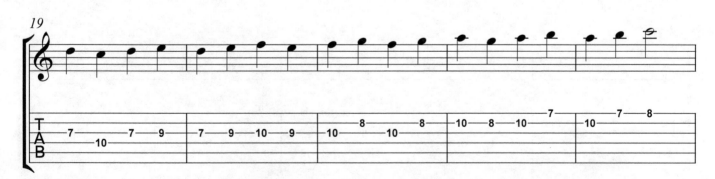

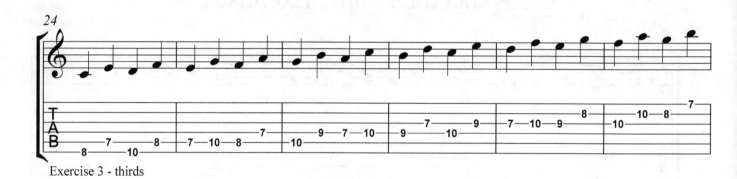

Exercise 3 - thirds

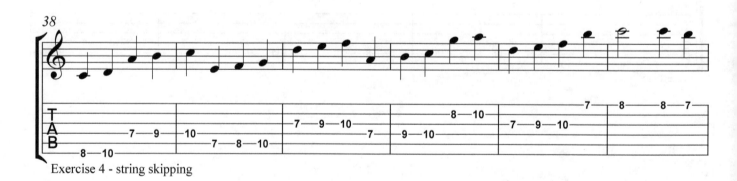

Exercise 4 - string skipping

Diatonic Scales
(Extended Forms)

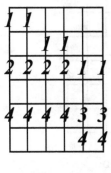 Ionian (major) 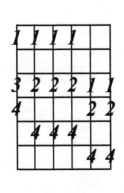 Dorian 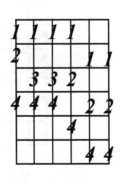 Phrygian 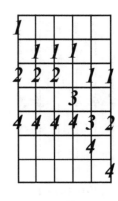 Lydian

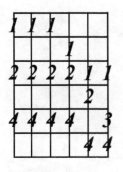 Mixolydian 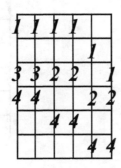 Aeolian (minor) 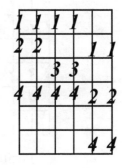 Locrian

Key of...	C	G	D	A	E	B	F#	C#	Ab	Eb	Bb	F
Ionian	8	3	10	5	12	7	2	9	4	11	6	13
Dorian	10	5	12	7	2	9	4	11	6	13	8	3
Phrygian	12	7	2	9	4	11	6	1	8	3	10	5
Lydian	13	8	3	10	5	12	7	2	9	4	11	6
Mixolydian	3	10	5	12	7	2	9	4	11	6	13	8
Aeolian	5	12	7	2	9	4	11	6	1	8	3	10
Locrian	7	2	9	4	11	6	13	8	3	10	5	12

Blues Scales

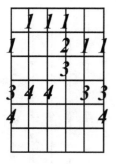

Position 1

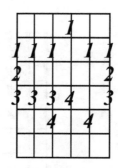

Position 2

Position 3

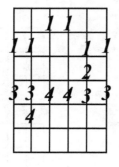

Position 4

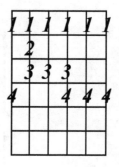

Position 5

Position 5 is the blues scale that most people are familiar with, and it's very similar to the minor pentatonic scale. The other scales (positions 1-4) have a lot of similarities to their pentatonic scale counterparts, but the patterns are a little different because of the way the notes are scattered.

Key of...	C	G	D	A	E	B	F#	C#	Ab	Eb	Bb	F
Position 1	8	3	10	5	12	7	2	9	4	11	6	13
Position 2	10	5	12	7	2	9	4	11	6	13	8	3
Position 3	12	7	2	9	4	11	6	1	8	3	10	5
Position 4	3	10	5	12	7	2	9	4	11	6	13	8
Position 5	5	12	7	2	9	4	11	6	1	8	3	10

Extra Scales for Further Study

Harmonic Minor

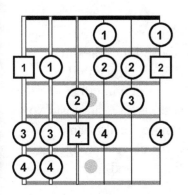

Formula: 1, 2, b3, 4, 5, b6, 7
Example: C, D, Eb, F, G, Ab, B

Use this to solo over min/maj 7 chords (i.e. R, b3, 5, 7) and also over ii-V-I progressions in minor keys (e.g. Bm7b5 - Em7 - Am7).
For faster chord changes, practice playing it in on octave patterns - sixth string to fourth string, and fourth string to first string.

Melodic Minor

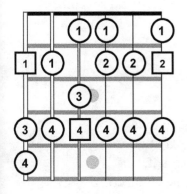

Formula: 1, 2, b3, 4, 5, 6, 7
Example: C, D, Eb, F, G, A, B

Use this to solo over min7 chords when you want a more jazzy sound.
For further study, try figuring out the different modes of this scale, which will give you the Lydian Dominant scale (mode 4) and the Altered Scale (mode 7).

Whole Tone

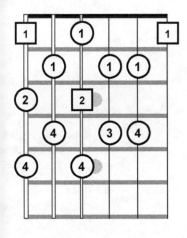

Formula: 1, 2, 3, #4, #5, b7
Example: C, D, E, F#, G#, Bb

Use this to solo over dominant 7 chords when you want a more jazzy sound. Try working on one octave versions of it so you can use it over quick chord changes. Also, there are only two versions of this scale because of the structure of it. If you play this scale starting on C#, that's the only other way to play this scale (C#, D#, F, G, A, B). If you start on a different note, you still get the same scale formula - all whole tones - so you can use it on any dominant 7 chord whose root note is in the scale.

Diminished

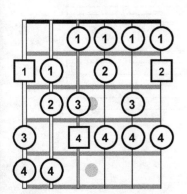

Formula: 1, 2, b3, 4, b5, #5, 6, 7
Example: C, D, Eb, F, Gb, G#, A, B

Use this to solo over diminished 7 chords, and practice both the one octave and two octave versions. This scale is based on a "whole-half step" repeating formula. There is also a "half-whole" diminished scale based on that kind of formula (half-whole) that can be used to solo over dominant 7 chords.

Arpeggios

Arpeggios are like miniature scales based on specific chords. When you play a G7 chord, you're playing at least four notes - G, B, D, and F. To play a G7 arpeggio, you find all instances of those four notes in a four to five fret span on the guitar, and use that scale-like pattern to improvise over that specific chord. Arpeggios are harder to use in improvisation because you spend less time on them before moving to a different pattern (typically one or two measures instead of eight to twelve) and the patterns have at most two notes per string, and often just one. However, mastering arpeggios allows you much more freedom in improvisation, because you can solo over any chord progression as long as you know the correct arpeggios. It also allows you to target specific chord tones during your solos, which will make them sound more musical.

The diagrams for the arpeggios are a little different from the scales. The note markers on the diagram are either a square, a white circle, or a black circle. The root note of the arpeggios and the octaves of the root note are marked by squares. The fifth tone is marked with a white circle, and then the third and seventh tones are marked with black circles.

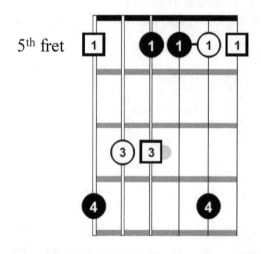

Min. 7 (Root 6)

5th fret

Also, in some cases you'll have to lay a finger across two strings to play the pattern. In the diagram to the left, this is indicated by the straight line connecting the note played by the first finger on the third string and the adjacent note on the second string.

And it would be played as follows:

Major 7th Arpeggios

I included a root 3 arpeggio for this group because the root 6 arpeggio that starts on the fourth finger has a huge stretch in the first 4 notes, no matter how you arrange the fingering.

Major 7 (Root 6)

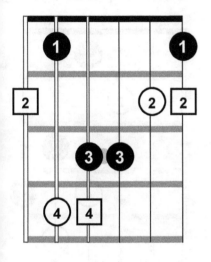

Major 7 (Root 5)

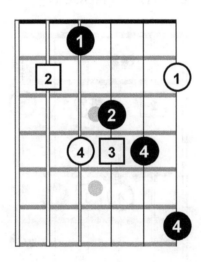

Major 7 (Root 4)

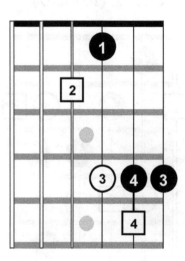

Major 7 (Root 5)

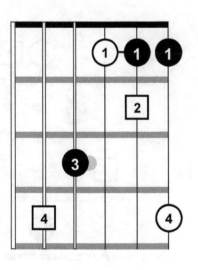

Major 7 (Root 4)

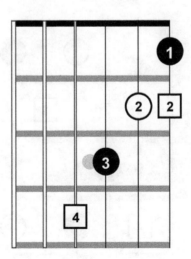

Major 7 (Root 3)

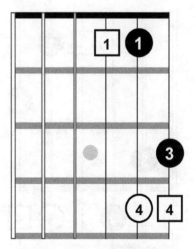

Dominant 7th Arpeggios

These can be incorporated into pentatonic soloing, especially in blues songs. Try using the first root 6 arpeggio over a minor pentatonic scale. For example, if you're using a G minor pentatonic scale for a blues in G (G, C, and D progression), use the first root 6 arpeggio starting at the third fret (G). Even though there are some notes that don't overlap, it will sound good switching between the arpeggio and the scale.

Dom. 7 (Root 6)

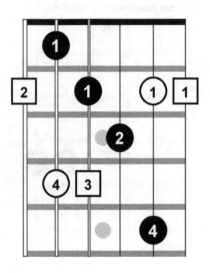

Dom. 7 (Root 5)

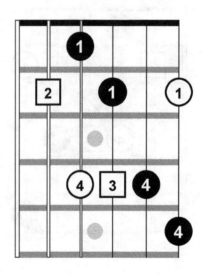

Dom. 7 (Root 4)

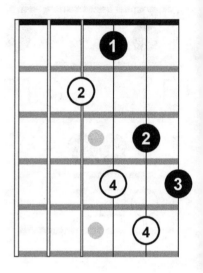

Dom. 7 (Root 6)

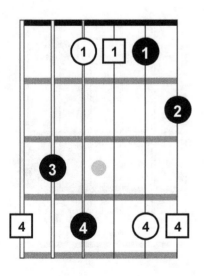

Dom. 7 (Root 5)

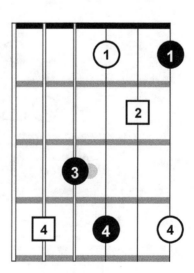

Dom. 7 (Root 4)

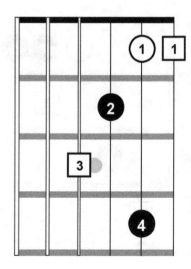

Minor 7th Arpeggios

These are really useful to learn and incorporate into pentatonic solos. You can easily see the similarity between the first root 6 arpeggio and the minor pentatonic scale. The first root 5 arpeggio is similar to the position 3 pentatonic scale, and the second root 6 arpeggio is similar to the position 4 pentatonic scale.

Min. 7 (Root 6)

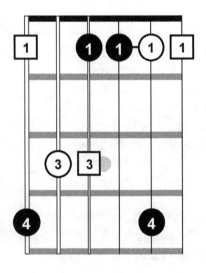

Min. 7 (Root 5)

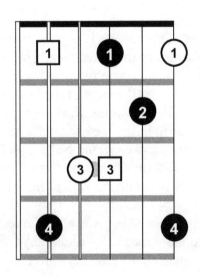

Min. 7 (Root 4)

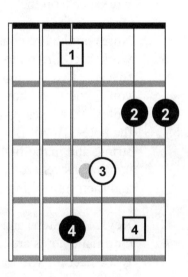

Min. 7 (Root 6)

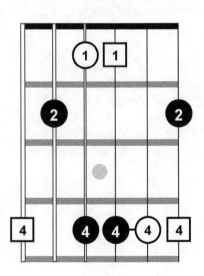

Min. 7 (Root 5)

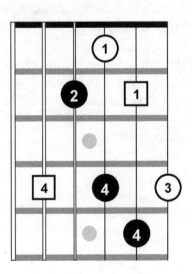

Min. 7 (Root 4)

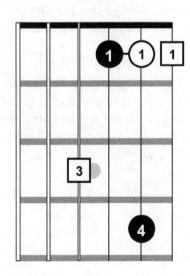

Theory Section

This next section is going to give you some information about music theory as it relates to guitar. Since music theory is such a large subject, this section will only focus on the basics such as the names of the notes and how keys are constructed. Here are instructions on how to fill out the worksheets on the pages that follow.

Notes on the Fretboard Worksheet: This page tells you the twelve note names, and has a worksheet for you to fill out the names of the notes on all six strings from frets one through twelve. This is important to know so when you're tuning your guitar, if it's really out of tune you'll know just how out of tune it is. At the back of the book is a page called "Chromatic Notes" that gives you the answers. To fill out the worksheet, first try to memorize the names of the notes (A, A#/Bb, etc.), and then fill in the boxes underneath each string. Start with the sixth string, and in the first box the correct answer would be "F", and then in the box under that, the correct answer would be "F#/Gb." Continue with the rest of the notes until you reach the end, and then start filling in the names of notes on the fifth string, and then the rest of the strings.

Keys, Half Steps and Whole Steps: This page gives a brief overview of how the twelve chromatic notes are arranged into more musically useful keys and scales. The page after it is a worksheet for you to test your knowledge of how keys are constructed. At the end of the book is a page with the correct answers.

Intervals: This page shows common intervals, some of which you might use in guitar solos or songs. An interval is a pair of notes played either simultaneously, like a miniature chord, or sequentially.

Chord Diagram - Tab Exercise: This page is a worksheet for those of you who need a little extra work getting familiar with reading tablature. Take the string/fret information from each chord diagram and write out the chord in the tablature staff below, remembering that you don't write down any information about what fingers to use in tablature. A few of the chords have been done for you, and the answers are on the page called "Chord Chart" at the back of the book.

Musical Symbols: This page shows you some of the common musical symbols used in standard notation including notes, rests, and various kinds of repeat symbols and bar lines. For a full explanation of this subject, either get a book that focuses on standard notation, or contact a local guitar teacher for a few lessons.

Notes on the Fretboard Worksheet

The 12 notes in the Chromatic scale are:
A A#/Bb B C C#/Db D D#/Eb E F F#/Gb G G#/Ab
Fill these in the blank spots in the chart below starting with the open note for each string.

Open	Sixth E	Fifth A	Fourth D	Third G	Second B	First E
1st Fret						
2nd						
3rd						
4th						
5th						
6th						
7th						
8th						
9th						
10th						
11th						
12th						

Keys, Half Steps and Whole Steps

First, some definitions . . .

1) <u>Half Step</u>: The distance from one note on the chromatic scale to the next one (e.g. from A to A♯/B♭).
2) <u>Whole Step</u>: The distance from one note on the chromatic scale to second note up (e.g. from A to B, or from C♯ to D♯)
3) <u>Tonic</u>: The tonal center of a key, and also the first note of a scale.
4) <u>Key</u>: A fixed group of notes picked from the chromatic scale to facilitate composition or improvisation. One note is considered the tonal center of the group (i.e. the "Master" note), and all other notes in the group are considered subordinate to that note. The key is also named after the note that is the tonal center. This group of notes is then used to generate scales and chords which are practiced on musical instruments to use in composition and improvisation.
5) <u>Scale</u>: A series of notes arranged in order from lowest to highest in pitch. Scales are memorized and practiced on instruments and are used to create melodies.
6) <u>Chord</u>: A collection of three or more notes played simultaneously to support and enhance a melody. Songs usually consist of melodies and chord changes; in some cases songs consist of only melodies (a capella singing, for example) and more rarely just chord changes (mood music in a movie soundtrack would be one of the few uses for this type of song).

Most of the music you have listened to is written using a major or minor key. We're going to learn about the major key.

Major keys are derived from the chromatic scale by picking one of the notes as the tonic and then selecting the other six by going up in a series of whole steps and half steps. The chromatic notes, formula, and an example are below.

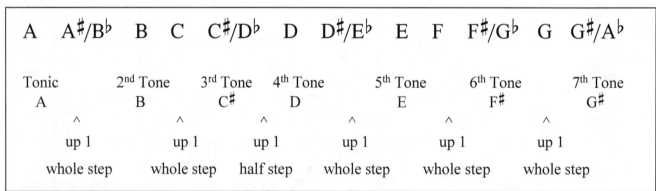

Going up another half step would bring you back to the A note, but up one octave from where you started. All other keys follow this same formula, and there are 12 keys that with which songs can be written. One rule that is followed when deciding whether to use a sharp note or a flat note, is that you never skip a letter, and you never repeat a letter. So in this case, we used C♯ instead of D♭, because we would have skipped the letter C and used the letter D twice.

The 12 keys are C, G, D, A, E, B, F♯, (or G♭), C♯ (or D♭), A♭, E♭, B♭, and F. Using this formula, see if you can figure out what notes are in each one.

Key Worksheet

Key of . . .

I	ii	iii	IV	V	vi	vii	viii
C							
G							
D							
A	B	C♯	D	E	F♯	G♯	A
E							
B							
F♯							
C♯							
A♭							
E♭							
B♭							
F							

Chromatic and Diatonic Intervals

Minor Second
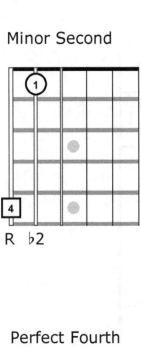
R ♭2

Major Second
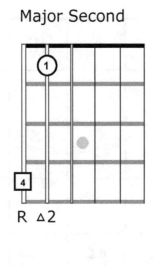
R △2

Minor Third
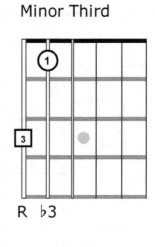
R ♭3

Major Third
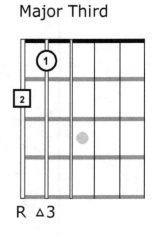
R △3

Perfect Fourth
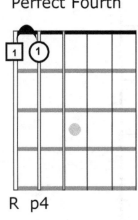
R p4

Aug. 4th/Dim. 5th
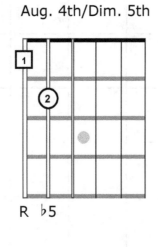
R ♭5

Perfect 5th (Power Chord)
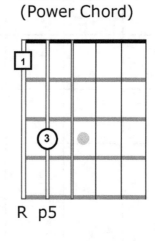
R p5

Aug. 5th/Min. 6th
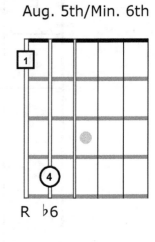
R ♭6

Major Sixth
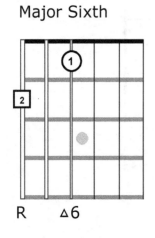
R △6

Minor 7th
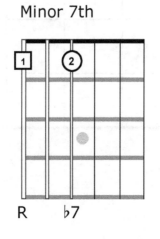
R ♭7

Major 7th
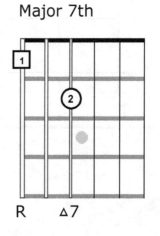
R △7

Octave
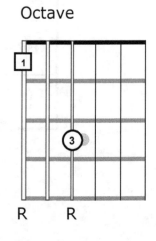
R R

Chord Diagram - Tab Exercise

If you want to get better at reading tablature, try to translate the information in the chord diagrams to the tablature staff. A few have been done for you, and the answers are in the page called "Chord Chart" near the back of the book.

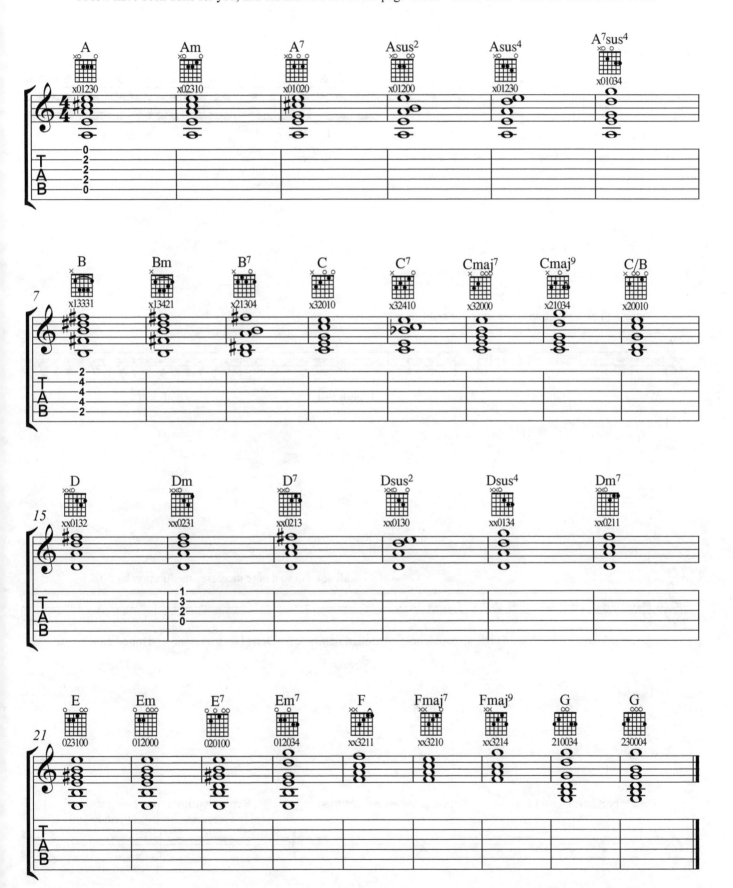

47

Musical Symbols

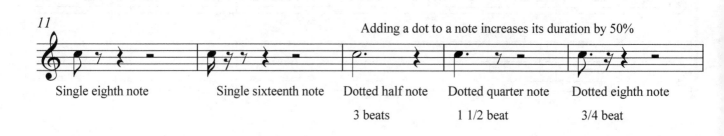

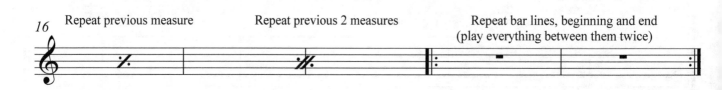

Chromatic Notes

A A#/B♭ B C C#/D♭ D D#/E♭ E F F#/G♭ G G#/A♭

	Sixth	Fifth	Fourth	Third	Second	First
Open	E	A	D	G	B	E
1st Fret	F	A#/B♭	D#/E♭	G#/A♭	C	F
2nd	F#/G♭	B	E	A	C#/D♭	F#/G♭
3rd	G	C	F	A#/B♭	D	G
4th	G#/A♭	C#/D♭	F#/G♭	B	D#/E♭	G#/A♭
5th	A	D	G	C	E	A
6th	A#/B♭	D#/E♭	G#/A♭	C#/D♭	F	A#/B♭
7th	B	E	A	D	F#/G♭	B
8th	C	F	A#/B♭	D#/E♭	G	C
9th	C#/D♭	F#/G♭	B	E	G#/A♭	C#/D♭
10th	D	G	C	F	A	D
11th	D#/E♭	G#/A♭	C#/D♭	F#/G♭	A#/B♭	D#/E♭
12th	E	A	D	G	B	E

Key Worksheet

Key of . . .

I	ii	iii	IV	V	vi	vii	viii
C	D	E	F	G	A	B	C
G	A	B	C	D	E	F♯	G
D	E	F♯	G	A	B	C♯	D
A	B	C♯	D	E	F♯	G♯	A
E	F♯	G♯	A	B	C♯	D♯	E
B	C♯	D♯	E	F♯	G♯	A♯	B
F♯	G♯	A♯	B	C♯	D♯	E♯	F♯
C♯	D♯	E♯	F♯	G♯	A♯	B♯	C♯
A♭	B♭	C	D♭	E♭	F	G	A♭
E♭	F	G	A♭	B♭	C	D	E♭
B♭	C	D	E♭	F	G	A	B♭
F	G	A	B♭	C	D	E	F

Chord Chart

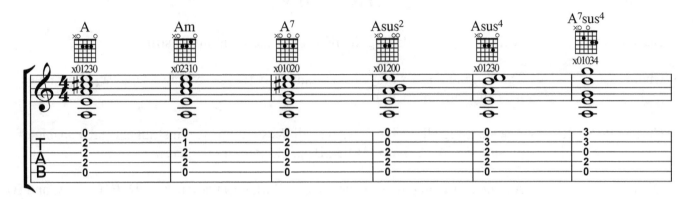
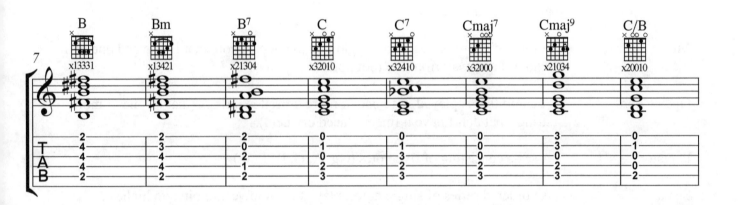
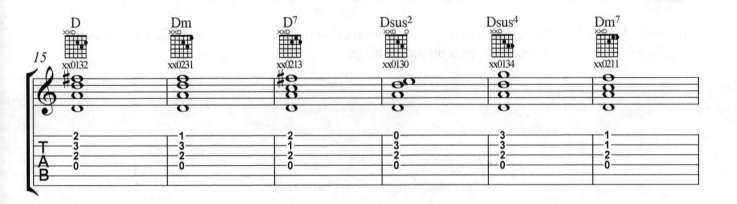
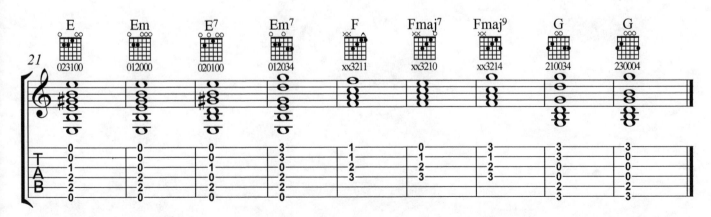

Glossary

Barre Chord	A chord played by laying the first finger across multiple strings.
Chord	Three or more notes played simultaneously (note – when you play a pair of notes it's called an "interval").
Chromatic Scale	A scale using all twelve notes that all Western musical instruments are capable of playing (i.e. A, A sharp / B flat, B, C, C sharp / D flat, etc)
Diatonic	A scale consisting of seven notes (e.g. C Major Diatonic = C, D, E, F, G, A, and B)
Major	A kind of chord, scale, or arpeggio that includes a note that is two whole steps away from the root note.
Minor	A kind of chord, scale, or arpeggio that includes a note that is one and one half whole steps away from the root note.
Open Chord	A chord that is played with one or more unfretted strings (that is, one or more strings that don't have a finger placed on them).
Pentatonic	A scale consisting of five notes (e.g. A, C, D, E, G).
Scale	An ordered series of single notes, played from lowest in pitch to highest.
Standard Notation	Traditional musical writing, with oval note heads, treble clefs, etc.
Tablature (or "tab")	Newer form of musical notation using lines to represent strings, and numbers to represent frets on those strings.

CPSIA information can be obtained
at www.ICGtesting.com
Printed in the USA
LVHW01s1723170618
581007LV00032B/1647/P